This book gives a brief background of the author and his valuable childhood lessons and experiences which gave him the strength to rise above the past. It is designed to help young people growing up in the inner city to realize that there are so many things right there in the neighborhood that can help them in an urban setting. A little like an "it's what you make of it" approach. It will also help young readers to take advantage of what positive things are available in the neighborhood that can really help them survive what people call today "the Hood." The author also shares some bad decisions he made as a youth to help a young reader see he was not perfect and was affected greatly by a lot of the negative surroundings. The author shares how each experience was a lesson learned for him and how he still lives by these principles today. The book spares readers of all the drugs and serious violence that are glorified in movies and videos today. The goal is to help a young reader see that entertainment is not the only answer to making it out of an urban setting.

DOUSEY–N-EM
The Boys Club—My Bridge to Manhood

Sam Reynolds

authorHOUSE®

AuthorHouse™
1663 Liberty Drive
Bloomington, IN 47403
www.authorhouse.com
Phone: 1-800-839-8640

First published by AuthorHouse 4/26/2010

ISBN: 978-1-4520-1278-0 (e)
ISBN: 978-1-4520-1277-3 (sc)

Library of Congress Control Number: 2010905336

Printed in the United States of America
Bloomington, Indiana

This book is printed on acid-free paper.

Contents

Introduction

We hear too often about the horrors and hard times of those who grew up in the inner cities and low-income urban areas. Violence, guns, robberies, murders, and drugs are common practices in these areas, and that's just a plain fact. Of course, those of us who grew up in these areas do not like being stereotyped or prejudged because we experienced these things firsthand.

But if that's all we talk about in order to impress people or use it to make excuses for not doing what we know to be right, what can we expect? I notice that there are many positive things that happen in the urban areas that are often left out. These are the things I believe will help people to understand what is really happening in these urban settings and to be less judgmental toward those who are caught up in them.

In this book I would like to share some brief life experiences growing up in Newport News that I hope will help young individuals see that it is possible to survive the "hood," as most people call it today, without living up to all the negative stereotypes about us. And you do not need any exceptional talent. I'm always glad to hear about those who, because of their athletic ability or other talent, made it in the entertainment world. I'm always bragging about these individuals, especially those who come from Newport News, Virginia, or the Tidewater area. Some of these individuals put Newport News on the map. But there are some who did not possess these special talents who were able to get past the past and went on to become what people call model citizens and who are a great asset to their communities. Today I'm just your average Joe who, after graduating from high school, joined the military and then graduated from a junior college. I now work every day as a test engineer in the Space Department at a college laboratory. I've been married to a lovely woman for over twenty years and have two children who are adults. I'm very active in my Christian faith and in the community. I know that things may be far worse or better in the urban areas compared to when I was growing up, but I'm sure any young person who is having related experiences today can see that it's possible to get past the past if he or she really pays attention to what's happing in the neighborhood as lessons learned that can help later in life. This book certainly cannot do for people what God's word can do for any young person living in any area. I just hope it will help.

After I share some experiences with the reader, I go on to mention in or at the end of each chapter some lessons that I learned from these experiences, and especially from some of the real people in the neighborhood whom most people wouldn't give the time of day to. One other positive I would like to express in this publication is HRBC, which is an acronym for a boys' club located in the East End section of Newport News, Virginia. Today it is a Boys and Girls Club, but then HRBC was the acronym for Hampton Roads Boys Club. If you were to ask anyone growing up in the neighborhood at that time what HRBC stood for, though, they would tell you "Hard Running Black Children." Some of my story will explain why.

Everyone has a story to tell, especially those raised up in hard times. And like everyone else, I tell mine often. The problem I was having was that most individuals would find the story I told hard to believe. I was starting to wonder how far off from what really happened I deviated; of course, there will be some exaggeration. But every time I would return to my hometown in Newport News, it reminded me that I was only telling half the story, and I did not exaggerate much, if any at all. It still amazes me how much I experienced in life in this small city. The people, the culture, and the surroundings helped me with the only two things I feel that I have going for me—understanding people and becoming close to God.

Though I will reflect on all of my past in this book, I will focus mainly on the years from age twelve to fifteen. You're probably saying, "this guy must be kidding." Most people just ignore this time period in their lives and profess that their high school or college years made them what they are today. But I came to realize that everything I experienced in life and the way I handled myself after the age of eighteen was a result of what I dealt with during the middle school years. It probably was the most testing and challenging time for me. There were some trying times during my earlier childhood years, but they were nothing compared to later. The years I spent in the military (peacetime), college in my later years, marriage, raising children, and all the jobs I have worked were a walk in the park compared to those years. Never before or since, have I felt so close to dying from being harassed and from fights in turf wars with other housing projects. Although the East End section is relatively small, I was surrounded by every possible evil you can imagine from any large inner-city area.

I will be excluding most of the really bad experiences, because I do not believe it is necessary to mention them for those who have lived or are currently living in an urban setting to see how I was able to rise above these circumstances to make my life positive. If the reader's background is similar, he will be able to tell from the benign experiences I am relating that I'm only sharing a fraction of everything that takes place in these areas. The amazing and mostly humorous thing about this story is how I survived with those positive things I experienced, including God, my parents, my brother and sister, some close associates and friends, and as I mentioned earlier the Hampton Roads Boys Club (HRBC).

One particular individual who was a close friend but lived on a different block in the neighborhood will be mentioned by name often because of our related experience in the neighborhood and our membership together at HRBC. I decided to title this book after the team he created.

From Birth to Age Nine

I was born in New Haven, Connecticut, in 1961. I had one sister a year older and a brother two years younger than I. My father was from Lexington, Virginia, and my mother was from Newport News, Virginia. My parents moved to New Haven in the late fifties. I remember my parents having a hard time making a living. Two things while living in New Haven I will never forget: my father being a womanizer, and my mother having a nervous breakdown. Because of my father's constant thing with the ladies, my mother decided to move back to her hometown of Newport News during the summer of 1970.

Because my mother did not have a job or a place to stay, we children were divided up between relatives. My sister lived with one of my mother's sisters, who had one daughter about the same age and two sons. My mother and brother stayed with her mother; and I stayed with one of her other sisters, who had three boys, the youngest of which was a year older than I. At the end of the summer, my mother was able to find a two-bedroom house for us to live in. She received financial aid (welfare) until she was able to find work. My father would show up periodically and help out with some bills. He tried to work things through with my mother; I knew, even at that age, that he really loved her. My father was very handsome, but very weak when it came to women. I do have to say that some of the affairs he had were because of the very aggressive approach of some women.

Jim Crow South

I started the fourth grade at Booker T. Washington elementary school. During that particular school year, I kept feeling that there was something really different about the schools in the South—besides everyone talking with a strange accent. It wasn't until the end of the school year that I first realized what it was. One day during recess, I saw a little white girl (she looked white) playing in the school yard. That's when it hit me. She was the first and only white person I had seen in the school. As a matter of fact, she was the first white person I had seen since moving to Newport News. Virginia was still weaning itself from Jim Crow.

My first real challenge was trying to figure out why my fourth-grade teacher hated me so much. She was one of those I-don't-play-and-you-can-tell-your-parents-I-said-so type of teachers. She would look for every opportunity to spank me, which was okay for teachers to do back then in the South. I was extremely frightened when I saw her take the belt off of one of my classmates and start spanking him in front of the class. I made sure that I would not give this lady any reason to do the same to me. One day she felt that she finally had her chance to do so.

When she would leave the class for a short period, she would give us instructions about not talking. One day when she stepped out for a moment, the class was really in a chattering mode. Up until this time, I had not made any close friends. So I would just sit there and listen to everyone else talk. Normally the class was very good about becoming quiet just before she would walk back into the classroom. But this day, because the class was unusually loud, no one heard her walking back down the hall. When she came in the classroom, everyone got quiet. She then asked who was talking. Some of the kids in the class decided to let me be the scapegoat and pointed me out. The thing that surprised me the most was that she believed them.

She asked me to come to the front of the class and remove my belt. I pleaded with her that I was not talking and that I would not give her my belt. She then tried to grab my belt. I pushed her hand away. She tried to grab me again, but I put my foot behind her leg and pushed her to the ground. She got up and tried to grab me again. I did the same thing again. After the third time, she tried to hold on to me and keep her balance, but she fell and hit the floor again, this time with me on top of her. I got off her and asked her to please leave me alone. But she kept on coming, and I just kept on flipping. After I flipped her several more times, she realized she needed to keep me from putting my foot behind her. She then was able to wrestle me to the door. By this time she was very exhausted, her blouse was open and you could see her bra, and her wig was half twisted off her head. Holding me tight, she asked if I wanted to go to the principal's office. I told her no. She then asked me to return to my seat and to stop talking. I just said okay and started walking back to my desk.

As I walked, I noticed that the classroom was a mess. All my classmates were standing around the room against the wall with looks of disbelief on their faces, and maybe seven or eight desks were turned over. The teacher walked out of the room to go and fix herself up. While she was doing this, I decided to pick up the overturned desks and line them back up the way they were before. The rest of the class just stared at me like I was the creature from the black lagoon. The class really liked her, especially the girls. When she returned to the class, she just started teaching normally, like nothing ever happened.

Those little flirty looks I used to get from girls when the school year started had turned to looks of disgust. But I started to make good friends with the guys who at first had wanted to fight me. For about two weeks, the teacher seemed to be very mellow and laid-back. The class would cut up when she left the classroom, and when she returned she would calmly ask everyone to take their seats. She really seemed to be a changed person.

One day at the end of class, she asked me to stay behind for a few minutes. She started out talking about the scuffle we had gotten into and went on to say that she had not felt that she was in control of her class. She then said that for the past few weeks she had been taking judo classes and that she wanted to go another round if I felt I should disobey any commands given by her. I told her that I did not want to fight her again. She then said that she now felt she was back in charge of her class. The very next day she was back to her normal self. I was sort of glad she was. From that day on, we became very close; I had become one of her favorite students. I also found out later why she did not care for me at first. It was because of my New England accent.

From the experience with my fourth-grade teacher, I learned to really pay attention to what people are saying. She never said that she was going to hit me with the belt. I learned later that she would always ask for your belt but would never hit any of the kids with it. In the sixth grade, I had a similar experience with my science teacher. When he left the class one day, a fight broke out in class and I tried to break it up. When the teacher came back, he thought I was part of helping someone gang up on the others. He pulled me out and slung me over one of the desks. I got up and walked toward him with this I'm-going-to-do-to-you-what-I-did-to-my-fourth-grade-teacher attitude. While he was bending over picking up one of the chairs, I punched him in the nose. He grabbed me by the collar and slammed me on the lab table. He raised his fist in the air to strike me, and if it had not been for half of the class grabbing him, he would have killed me. He was over six feet tall compared to my barely five-foot-tall fourth-grade teacher. From this experience, I learned a second lesson: never fight a teacher.

That next year the city enforced busing, and once again I was attending an integrated school. Of course, this was normal for me. But it was a new experience for me to see how whites and blacks were reacting to this change. This elementary school was really nice. It had been one of the all-white schools at first. My fifth-grade teacher, who before busing taught at an all-black elementary school, also taught my mother when she was in the fifth grade.

THE MOVE TO DICKERSON COURT

Halfway through the school year when I was ten years old, things really started to get tough financially for my mom. She decided to move to the East End area of Newport News in the housing project called Dickerson Court. This is where it all began for me. And that is what it really means to grow up in hard times. We were really poor before moving to Dickerson Court, but never had I been teased so much by others who were just as poor as we were and I had never gotten into any fights about it until now. Why was it so important to be loyal to your friends even if it meant doing jail time for them? I also wondered how I was going to live here without doing any jail time at all.

This section of Newport News when I was growing up was called "The Bottom." Do I need to explain why? After I left Newport News, it was this area that gave the entire city the name "Bad News." Dickerson Court was one of the oldest housing projects in downtown Newport News. It covered the entire 500 block, running from Seventeenth to Twenty-Second Street. By the time I was in my early teens, it was one of the toughest places for a young person to grow up in Newport News. Lasister Court, Ritley Circle, Harbor

Homes, and others had their rough spots, but nothing like Dickerson Court. It had the normal internal and external appearances of an urban project area. On the perimeter of the area, you would see people standing around talking, smoking cigarettes, and being discreet about smoking a marihuana cigarette or drinking alcohol, which was a fifth of something or a quart of malt liquor. As you walked through the neighborhood, you would at times see people rolling dice or pitching pennies a fight here and there. But the sports activities would most of the time overshadow these negative things. Most of us were on the basketball court or on the softball or football field playing sandlot tackle.

The families living in Dickerson Court were very close. Many were single-parent families, with mostly mothers being head of the household. Not all the single mothers were a result of deadbeat fathers. Many fatherless families in Dickerson Court at the time were a result of men killed in the Vietnam War. Then you had those men who were incarcerated for breaking the law trying to provide for their families. Like most housing projects, we would have our own issues and differences with each other. It could be really dangerous for someone not from Dickerson Court to come into the neighborhood and start trouble.

The new school I had to attend was located in the north Newport News area called Deer Park. My fifth-grade teacher was white and was meaner than my fourth-grade teacher. I thought she was going to be really nice because she was so much younger than both teachers I had since living in Virginia. She was very pretty and reminded me of my second-grade teacher in New Haven, who was also white but very nice to all the students in the class. This new teacher made it clear that she had a serious problem with busing and integrating the schools. She was extremely nice to the white students. I thought maybe since I sounded so much like them, I would be treated a little better, but she hated me more for it. It didn't take much for us to upset her. Whenever we did something she did not like, she would send us to the back of the class and make us do the dead cockroach. You would lie on the floor on your back with both hands and feet sticking up in the air like a dead bug. The white kids would pretend they had bug spray and said they were exterminating us. I just completely refused to do this. Those who did not comply were sent to the principal's office. The principal was black. When I came into her office, she would ask if my fifth-grade teacher had sent me there. When I said yes, she just smiled and told me to take a seat until the end of the school day.

Back in the neighborhood, just in the first week, I saw more fights than I had ever seen in my life, including what I had seen on television. What I was trying to get used to also was the fact that these were black-on-black fights. Back at Booker T. Washington, I did not see one fight in school (not counting the one my fourth-grade teacher and I got into) and only one fight in the neighborhood. The other fights before we moved were white versus black fights in school. At Deer Park, there was a fair-complexioned girl in my class whose face was scratched up so bad by a darker-complexioned girl that I starting crying. This was my first experience with the hatred blacks had among ourselves. When I asked someone why the darker girl would do something like that, they said it was because she was a red bone. This was a term used about blacks or African-Americans with fair or lighter skin complexions. This was the first time I heard this expression. What troubled me even more was that I was just as light as she was, maybe slightly darker. I knew my time was coming. I would see all of the new friends I met get into a fight within a week of my knowing them. It didn't matter how nice a person they were or how much they would try to avoid trouble. Since I knew my time was coming, I started taking notes on those who I saw could handle themselves very well.

The day finally arrived. After the school year was over, I had advanced to the sixth grade. During the summer I was out playing basketball over at the schoolyard where I would be attending grade six. By this time I had made a few friends. My closest friend at this time was James. Everyone in the neighborhood called him Possum. Possum was the youngest of six in his family. He had one brother and four sisters. The sister that was next older than him was really nice. She was a cheerleader or on the dance team, and we loved when her friends came to visit. The next older sister seemed to be really mean, at least to him. Every time she threatened to beat Possum, she would always include me in the equation. But when she actually whooped on Possum, she never really did anything to me. Man, I thought my sister was mean. Possum's sister was a few years older than he and had a reputation for being a good fighter, even beating up on guys her age. Poor Possum didn't have a chance. Of course, things changed after he had gotten a little older.

My sister Pam was only a year older than I, so she never was able to push me around. If we had the same age difference as Possum and his sister, I would have been in worse trouble than he. Getting back to the basketball court, Possum and I were playing with some other guys our age and a little older. There was one guy named Todd who was very light-skinned, and as in most inner-city areas he was called "white boy." I could tell from earlier run-ins that he wanted to nuck. Nucking was the term we used for fighting. While playing basketball, he kept making fun of the way I was talking. I still had that New England accent. Finally I just got tired of it and grabbed him and flipped him to the ground the same as I did my fourth-grade teacher. As he sat

10

on the ground, I charged at him. He grabbed me by the legs and picked me up—now he was over me. I could tell I was much stronger, so I was able to wrestle my way out from his hold and was about to really start folding him up. But some of the guys standing around decided to break up the fight. I really wanted to continue. He just looked at me and laughed about it. The next day, word had gotten out that he kicked my butt. I was so mad, and every time I saw him I wanted a rematch, because I knew I could take him. But he would just avoid the confrontation.

Believe it or not, we ended up becoming best friends. Todd, Possum, and I were like brothers. I then learned Todd was the youngest of four. He had one older brother and two older sisters. Like Possum, Todd also had a sister a few years older than he that whooped up on him occasionally.

Real People in the Neighborhood

There were so many different types of personalities that stood out in the neighborhood. I would like to mention some of these individuals because, believe it or not, they were part of the forces that shaped me. Some of these individuals by today's standards were basically homeless, but most of us at the time did not see them that way. For example, there was a bag lady that pushed a shopping basket full of fruits and vegetables tossed in the dumpster by the local grocery stores. She would sell them in the neighborhood. We called her Biscuit. I have no idea where that name came from, but the youths would address her as Ms. Biscuit. She always had my respect because she had her own business and seemed to be doing well. Of course, I was still in grade school at the time. One day when I saw how she was receiving her produce, I tried to warn a friend whose mother purchased some tomatoes from Ms. Biscuit. The friend explained to me that everyone knew where she got the stuff; they would just buy it and then throw it away afterward. They respected the fact that she wasn't standing on the corner looking for a handout.

Another well-known personality in the neighborhood was a man that everyone called Pot. He walked around with a baseball bat, a three-foot-square checkerboard, and a bag of very large checkers. He constantly harassed the kids in the neighborhood.

There also was a man who had one of his eyes poked out and did not wear a mask to cover it. We called him One-Eye. One-Eye would stand on the corner of different blocks of Jefferson Avenue and make sexual advances at most of the women walking past him. It was said that one day, when he had two good eyes, he had asked a lady for some sex. She took her umbrella and poked him in the eye. Looking at his eye, I thought the story might be true, because it looks like the end of an umbrella could fit perfectly in the hole of the bad eye.

Behind one of the stores near the alley was an old man people called Turkey Tom. He, too, was a person who at that time I thought was a hardworking man with a respectable business. To this day I don't know how he got the name Turkey Tom. He lived in an abandoned warehouse space full of bicycles and bicycle parts. Anyone who wanted a bike for his or her child could go to Turkey Tom and buy one really cheap. If you were ready to get rid of your bike, you could take it to him and he would make you an offer. He was like a neighborhood pawnshop. And if your bike was stolen, there was a 90 percent chance that it was in his collection of bikes or parts. He knew most of the bikes he had were stolen. Whenever anyone came by to inquire about a missing bike, he would come out with this .22 pistol with a taped-up handle and ask you to leave him alone. He would always deny having a stolen bike, even when the person would point out his or her bike to him.

Then there was Eddie. Eddie thought he was a cloned Bruce Lee. He was so obsessed with Bruce that he would walk and even try to talk like him. He had Bruce's entire karate wardrobe, including the nunchucks and the shoes. He would just walk through the projects mimicking Bruce's facial expressions and gestures. I thought that he was just going through a phase and would return back to the Eddie we knew before *Chinese Connection* and the other Bruce Lee movies. Don't get me wrong: Bruce Lee had all of us karate-crazy, but Eddie took it to another level. And when Bruce died, Eddie became his imitator. He was Bruce up until I graduated and left for the military.

I attended an elementary school only a block away from where I lived. This was our hangout to do things we did not want our parents to know about. I'll talk about some of those things later. There was an older slim man who was a janitor at the school, and we called him Pregnant Pete. As thin as he was, he had the largest belly I had ever seen on a human being. He would chase us away every time we would try to hang out by the school during his working hours.

Now I want you to know that we addressed these people as Sir and Mister when we were in their face. But there were times that they would hear us calling them something other than that. You may find this hard to believe, but a person can learn a lot from these individuals by really reaching out and getting to know them and showing them the same respect he or she would like to receive. Before I graduated from high school, I would stop and converse with these individuals. I was always amazed at the wisdom a young person could receive from them about life. Some of their suggestions I still apply in life today. Some would demand respect, as was the case with Turkey Tom.

Truck Turner was another individual who demanded such respect. He was a gentleman in what seemed to us then his early sixties. He rode a large, late-fifties-style bicycle with a large basket in both the front and rear of the bike. We called these types of bicycles "trucks." Someone said that his name was Mr. Turner, so we named him after the 1974 blaxploitation film *Truck Turner*. The strange thing about Truck Turner was that you would always see him riding his bike at top speed through the neighborhood, coming and going in different directions. No one had any idea where he was going to or where he came from or why he was moving so fast. He would just sit straight up in his bicycle seat and pass though the neighborhood about four or five times a day. One day we were all standing around getting ready to play some basketball when we saw Truck Turner smash head-on into one of the housing project walls. We laughed so hard and loud that Truck Turner, after dusting himself off, came over to us and asked what we thought was so funny. No one wanted to answer him. After he asked the question for about the fifth time, a guy named Terrence said that we were all laughing at him running into the wall. Terrence then asked him what he was going to do about it. Truck Turner just picked up his bike and left.

We then started playing basketball as planned. About thirty minutes into our game, someone noticed Truck Turner riding toward us with that same look he always had on his face. "Terrence, here comes yo boy Truck Turner," someone said. As Truck Turner approached the court, he pulled out what appeared to be a .32-caliber pistol. He walked up to Terrence while we were playing, put the gun to his head, and asked Terrence if he still thought something was funny. Terrence ignored him and kept telling us not to worry and just keep playing ball. Finally Truck Turner stopped asking questions, got back on his bike, and continued on his normal bike route, which he continued to do until I left Newport

News. But, of course, we no longer addressed him as Truck Turner but as "Mr. Turner."

Other older people in the area also did what they thought would get the respect they felt they deserved from young people, even if it meant tossing dye (hot bleach) on us, or even poisoning us, not so much to kill us but just enough to make us very sick. Then I came to understand why my parents said we should respect our elders regardless of who they are—not only was it the God-fearing thing to do but also the safest.

A young person can learn so much from these types of individuals, as I did. Pot helped us to appreciate our parents' warnings about strangers. He would not have been able to roam the neighborhood as he did in a suburban setting. We really came to appreciate why our parents said that we should not use foul language when we heard Pot getting upset with someone. To this day, I have never heard anyone who could use curse words the way he did. Hearing him for about a minute was enough to shock a young person from using curse words for about a month. The worst part about it was he mostly was cursing us young people out. He would show the utmost respect for our parents and other adults in the neighborhood, and they would offer him a meal or two because he was so polite toward them. When our parents and other adults heard him cursing us out, they always took his side and thought that we were teasing him, which in most cases we were. But we learned early and not just from Pot, if you show respect toward those old enough to be your parents, it can benefit you in so many ways.

This was proven when I was fifteen years old. I would always show the utmost respect toward those old enough to be my parents. One day Todd and I let my brother and cousin ride our bikes. Later on in the day, he and I decided to go to the basketball court over by the school and stop by this clubhouse that we had built. When passing the court, we noticed our bicycles were lying on the ground near the school. We decided to walk over and see what was going on because my brother and cousin were nowhere in sight. Todd and I decided to pick our bikes up and ride them home. At this time a police officer came from around the school, and we noticed a police vehicle parked about thirty yards away from us. He told us to get off the bikes. We were trying to explain to the officer that the bikes belonged to us. He repeated his order, and Todd decided he would comply, but I said again that this bike belonged to me and I was about to take off riding. At this time the officer kicked me in the side, and I fell off the bike to the ground. I don't know what I was thinking of, but I was so angry that I started coming toward the cop. He reached for his revolver and told me to step back and start walking toward the police car.

Little did we know that some young people in the neighborhood saw this white cop kick me off my bike for what looked to them like no good reason. They were yelling in the neighborhood that a white cop kicked Junie Reynolds off his bike. While Todd and I were walking toward the car, we noticed that my brother and cousin were sitting in the back seat. The police officer asked us if we knew them. I told him it was my brother and cousin. He said when he asked them if they knew us, they told him no, so the officer thought we were trying to steal their bikes. He had them in the car because, as a result of there being so many break-ins, there was a strict law on how close a person could be to the school when it was closed,. My bother and cousin were just hanging around too close. The same thing could happen if you were playing handball on the side of the school.

By this time half of Dickerson Court, along with my mom, was walking toward the school. The officer immediately called for backup. You could see the fear on his face. Before we saw the crowd, we were thinking about just taking off running, but then we would have looked guilty to everyone else. The officer explained to my mother what had happened and he apologized as well. I thought my mom was still going to curse him out, but instead she asked me why I didn't get off the bike when he asked me; she then went on to get on my brother's and cousin's case. All my mother had to do was appear to be upset about what the officer had done, and trust me, it would have been a riot. Now you probably are wondering what this has to do with showing respect toward your elders. Trust me when I say this: if I had a reputation for being disrespectful toward adults in Dickerson Court, not one individual would have came to support me, only my mother. That cop could have treated us a lot worse and no one would have cared, but the crowd brought the officer, Todd, my brother, my cousin, and me to our senses, because we knew just how bad this could have gotten.

Now back to lessons learned from real people in the neighborhood. Individuals like Ms. Biscuit and Turkey Tom were entrepreneurs in their own right.

Truck Turner did not have a job or a business; he just always gave the impression that he was going somewhere important, minding his own business. I learned this was a good way to keep people from being suspicious of you. Whether you had a job or not, always give the impression that you were productive about something. I came to learn that there were many people who walked around sometimes in dress suits but didn't have a job. These were the last people the police would suspect of doing anything wrong compared to those who just stood around looking like they wanted trouble.

Eddie certainly taught us that a person can be whoever he wanted to be, plain and simple. We also learned something from how One Eye treated women. You may ask how. Well, when we saw how he would disrespect women, we at certain times thought this was real funny—until you heard him say the same thing to your mother or your sister, and then it was an entirely different ball game. Then we started to get on his case when he would harass any female, and we would chase him off the block. He and many of us learned to have respect for women, period.

Of course, there were many others who I call real people in the neighborhood, but I just wanted to mention a few. Most of these individuals were homeless, but they would always find a way to survive in those conditions without selling drugs, robbing people, or killing someone for no good reason. I figured that there had to be something positive a person could learn from them since I never saw them getting into trouble with the law.

Joining HRBC

I was really starting to get to know people in the neighborhood. By the time I was about eleven years of age, I had lost just about all my New England accent and was pretty much converted to the inner-city ways. All the goals and dreams about becoming a fighter pilot, an engineer, or a sports hero had just about completely left my mind. I was now focusing on how to make money quick and fast, perfecting my street-fighting skills, and finding my first girlfriend. Peer pressure had a very negative effect on many of us. Whether you lived in the suburbs or the city, experimenting with drugs and alcohol was something you'd better try.

By the time I was fifteen, I had a tattoo on each of my arms. These were the sewing needle, thread, and India ink type. The sad thing about the tattoos was that the girl I was trying to impress told me it was a sin to have them. Young men having an earring in their ear was starting to become popular. The old heads in the neighborhood still viewed this as a sissy thing to do. After my tattoo experience, I decided to pass on the earring idea. Numbing your ear with a clothespin or a cube of ice and getting punctured with a sewing needle was too much pain and no gain. These things were top priority for most people in the area.

I lived one block away from the Hampton Roads Boys Club (HRBC). I would always see individuals going there but never had an interest in joining. I decided one day to ask Todd about some of the things they did there. He said he had a membership card, which at that time only cost a buck annually. By the time he finished listing all the things a young person could do at the club, I was wondering why in the world we were hanging around in the streets when all this was going on. I did not know it at the time, but we had one of the best boys' clubs on the East Coast and maybe in the United States. It had some of the best directors you could imagine, like Mr. Pooh Johnson and others. Prominent sport figures would come to visit and make generous donations. The Club, or HRBC as we called it, had a full-size gymnasium. The basketball court had a modern scoreboard, bleachers that ran down one side of the gym, and a locker room. There was a game room with pool, ping-pong, hockey, and foosball tables. There was a lounge room where we could watch television. It also had a room where you could play checkers, cards, and chess. The other side of the Club had a library, study room, and another game room to play pinball machines. The sports program was organized and popular in the area. It had a trophy case for intramural leagues and when they played other boys' clubs and city recreation facilities. I decided to go and visit one day and could not believe my eyes. This club had so many activities going on. They would even take a group of those who were interested to the movie theater every week. I mean, all this was right in the middle of one of the toughest places to live in the city.

When I was in the seventh grade, my brother Douglas was in the fifth. He would always talk about this young guy in his class named Lawrence Richardson. They called him Dousey. Douglas would talk about his athletic skills and said that he was one of the best basketball players he had ever seen. I asked myself, *how good can a ten-year-old be?*

When I decided to join the Club, I had a chance to see what my brother was talking about. This young guy could indeed play. One day my brother formally introduced me to him. He was just in the fifth grade, so I was not too enthused about hanging out with him. I will be talking about Dousey often. Dousey was born in Newport News, Virginia. Like most of us, he was raised by a single mother. He started playing basketball at the age of four when he joined the HRBC. He started playing Little League football for the Club at age twelve. Dousey was born in a family of eleven, six boys and five girls. Although he had four older brothers, he was introduced to the Big Brothers program, a program that was designed to help inner-city youths receive mentoring from older volunteers. Dousey loved going to the Club.

Dousey put a group of us together as a team in three different sports: softball, football, and basketball. This group was instrumental in my learning about so many important values in life as a young person growing up in the inner city. I will be discussing this more later.

My brother also introduced me to two other classmates of his, two young girls who lived in the same housing project we did. Their names were Sandy and Carolyn. Sandy and Carolyn were not tomboys; they were a year or so younger than I. I always looked at them like younger sisters, but as they started getting older and developing more, we started looking at them a little different. As they developed during the teen years, they became some of the most attractive girls in Newport News, and I was already close friends of theirs. But before I had a chance to develop any interest in Sandy as far as dating her, she made it clear that she would never date anyone in the neighborhood, especially anyone living in Dickerson Court. I think she did have some interest in maybe one or two guys living in the area, but she was determined to live by this rule of hers. I just continued to treat her like a sister and a close friend.

Carolyn, on the other hand, did not have this same rule; she was a little more liberal, so I thought maybe I might have a chance with her, until I heard her say that she was partial toward guys with dark complexions. I was going to ask just how dark she was talking about. Or what was too light. I was frightened of what answer she might give. I never got the nerve to ask her, so I just felt I should move on and continue treating her like a sister and a friend as well. I picked up a lot of good habits from Sandy and Carolyn on how to treat people; I wish I could say I did the same for them. They really kept me from getting into so much trouble, especially when I thought I had to prove my manhood to someone. Carolyn had a way with words and was a very influential speaker. She could always find the right things to say to keep me and a lot of us from doing something really stupid. Sandy and Carolyn later became some of my closest friends, along with Todd and Possum.

The other two individuals who were part of our small group of friends were Al and Bobby, who moved to Newport News from North Carolina, where they grew up working on a farm; they were as strong as some of the mules they worked with. Bobby was a year younger than I, and Al was a year older. Al and I were in the same grade. They later became known for their fighting skills but mostly for their athletic abilities. I learned from these guys how to walk on my hands, do somersaults, and so many other things, including how to fight,. But once again it was the HRBC that kept us out of trouble.

I would like to make one other note about the light-skinned and dark-skinned dilemma. Al and Bobby were dark-skinned guys who got much attention from all the young girls in the neighborhood and in school. For the life of me, I can't understand to this day why so many dark-skinned people say they had a complex about their complexion. I can't tell you how many times I got dumped for a darker-complexioned person. I started to develop a complex because of my light skin. In time I started to become partial toward girls with darker skin. I remember a very beautiful young lady I really wanted to talk to. She just kept giving me a hard time when I asked her for a chance. Every time I saw her, I would tell her how beautiful she was. She could not believe I thought she was so pretty. Then she hit me with this "you think I'm pretty to be so dark, right?" comment. I just stared at her and told her that I thought she was beautiful because she was dark. She stared at me for about three minutes not saying a word. Then she said that no one had ever said anything like that to her before. Her eyes became watery, and she just said thanks and left me standing there.

I'm just making a note of my experience here in hopes that it may help shed some light on this dilemma in the black community. I'm still trying to understand this to this day. When I say dilemma, I mean "How can a race of people be so self-conscious of their skin complexion, when other races of people think all blacks look alike?" Some African-Americans think the light skin/dark skin issue started with slavery. I could understand this some, but it was still confusing to me during this time when blacks were treated the same by everyone else no matter what your skin tone was.

Most of the young guys in the neighborhood were receiving the same message from the streets, and that street intelligence was far superior to book knowledge. We were learning how to pitch pennies, roll dice, and play cards for money, betting on everything we did not agree on. This also at times included taking things that did not belong to us. We were not the break-into-someone's-home type or the steal-someone's-bicycle type either. Trust me: we had plenty of those types in the area. My brother and I were very creative. We would read a lot and try to make application of what we would read. This involved everything from building projects, drawing, and real inventions. At first we would not tell our friends what we were doing, for fear we would be called bookworms or trying to be like white boys. Some of these inventions included making our own toys since we could not afford to buy them. We would save cardboard boxes, Popsicle sticks, hangers, kite rope, and tape. We would build rockets, airplanes, and spaceships that we saw on television. These hobbies became pretty intense as we got older.

But the most important thing for every young man growing up in DC was that he had to know how to play sports. This was regardless of what your situation was at home or at school. For several reasons. First, it was a safer way to send a message to someone you really didn't care for than getting into a fistfight with them. Settling matters on a basketball court was one way to earn respect from what we may have thought was an enemy. Second, good athletic skills in any neighborhood is always a way to get people's respect. Third, it kept us out of trouble—and there was always the thought that you might one day get paid for it. Most of us really thought that if you had any chance of going to college, it would be from an athletic scholarship. Even the guys who seemed to have some peculiar mannerisms could play ball.

It was so competitive in our neighborhood that you could choose your team with your eyes closed and end up with a decent squad. But it was the Club that refined most of us because HRBC had one of the best-organized intramural leagues on the East Coast.

Dousey-n-Em (My First Basketball Season)

All of us started out playing for different teams. By the time I was in the eighth grade, Reynard was about a year older but in the same grade as I was (this was because my birthday was late in the year). He played with guys a lot older. He was tall for his age. There were three levels determined by age in the HRBC intramural league—Junior, Intermediate, and Senior. While I was playing in the junior league, Reynard (Nard) was playing intermediate. He decided he wanted to coach a junior league team. Reynard lived across from Dousey. He was close to him and knew he had very good basketball skills for his age. So between them, they decided to put together a junior team from individuals they knew.

Reynard approached me while Dousey was recruiting others. I have no idea how or what they used to decide who would be a good fit for the team. As I said earlier, most of the young boys in the neighborhood had at least a decent game. There were a few who were exceptional players, like Dousey. But there were many things that contributed to the success of our team, including the type of individuals we were and the good coaching from Nard Miller. I don't think any of us had any idea how good we would be as a team. We took on the name "Warriors" after the Philadelphia Warriors before the team changed its name to the 76ers. Most of us liked the team because of Dr. J (Julius Ervin), who used to play for the Virginia Squires before the ABA was dismantled. The Club used to take some of us to see the Squires play at the Hampton Coliseum.

Our first game together went so well and smooth, we started to think "maybe we got something here." We would beat our opponents by fifteen to twenty points or more. Some of these teams we thought were better than us. The word started to get around about how good we were, and each time we played, the gym became more packed, sometimes to the point where it was standing room only. After six or seven games into the season, we were no longer called the Warriors; people started calling us "Dousey-n-Em." He was the captain of the team. It was his skills that everyone came to see; he was also the youngest on the team. Dousey had a way of making all of us look good. For those of us who were decent, he had a way of taking us to the next level. We never argued or gave up in a game. We started to develop a lot of confidence in each other and Reynard as a coach. Dousey-n-Em became the talk in the neighborhood.

I remember one time Pooh Johnson arranged for us to play a boys' club from another area. This team was an all-white team. When they came in the gym, they could not believe that a gym like this would exist in an inner-city area. After the third period, we were up fifty to their nothing. We started to play a little lax, because some were starting to feel sorry for these guys. Others were starting to show a more militant, as we called it, attitude toward them. When either team would call time-out, you would hear someone say, "Let's blow these white boys away and not let them score." Some thought it would be a good thing or good sportsmanlike conduct to at least let these guys score two points. This was the first time our team became divided on any game we had played so far.

I was sort of ambivalent about what we should do. Race wasn't really the issue for me here; the side of me that wanted us not to let them score was the competitive side. If the other team was an all-black team or a diverse team, I would have still wanted to leave these guys with an egg for their score. I didn't want those who didn't want them to score to think that I had the same attitude as they had—and at the same time, I didn't want them to think I was feeling sorry for them, because as one player said, "If it was the other way around, do you think they would feel sorry for us and let us score?" But then there was the sportsmanship side that was taught to us at the Club that said we should indeed give these guys a break. We started to notice that the referees were calling cheap fouls on us to give them a chance to score. But they were about 0 for 10 or so at the free-throw line. We started to realize that in order for these guys to score, we would have to just let them run past us and get under the basket and shoot.

I forgot to mention that this game was on an early Saturday morning, not like our regular games in the evening in front of a sellout crowd. I'm sure these guys did not want to play in downtown Newport News in the evening, for which I do not blame them. But there were only about ten people watching the game. When there was about ten or fifteen seconds left in the game, some of us just let them pass the ball down the court and score right at the sound of the buzzer. Those who did not want them to score became very angry, and we started to hang our heads down while some seemed like they wanted to cry about it. The other team was so ecstatic they didn't get shut out that they started

31

jumping up and down and hugging the guy who made their only basket. They were waving their towels and hugging their coach. We could not believe our eyes. The final score was 69 to 2.

While all this was taking place, some individuals came in and saw the score, looked at us with our heads down, and then looked at them rejoicing like they won the national championship. Of course, they thought we got slaughtered by these guys. They immediately left the Club to spread the word that Dousey-n-Em got killed by some white guys from another boys' club. No one could believe it. What made things worse is when we were asked how we could let them do this, we thought they were talking about letting them score two points. We started pointing fingers. It took a while before everyone knew that we had really won the game. It's amazing that the only time we ever became divided was over race. After that, we never had differences again during or after a game.

At the end of the season, we were undefeated champions in the junior league. There was another team that was just as good and played us very well; some games they came very close to beating us. We would always come out victorious, though, sometimes with just seconds left on the clock. To be honest, I think if they just had a Dousey or maybe a coach like Nard, they probably would have beaten us. They were sort of like us—they played together well, and I can't remember them having any problems with each other.

Then came softball season. Reynard was so impressed with how we played together as a basketball team, he encouraged us to carry the same team over as a softball team. Some of us weren't all that enthused about playing softball, but we finally said "why not?" Halfway through the season, we were undefeated. By this time, we started to get a lot of attention and respect from our peers. This did so much for me because of my background. My family was probably the poorest in the projects, at least I thought so. This was why I thought the only thing I had going for me was not that I was good at sports, but just to be on a team that got so much respect from others. We ended up winning the softball championship.

When basketball season rolled around again, our team was fully established: me, Dousey, Bobby, Possum, and Johnny. It seemed that we would have a very good squad, but no one expected that we would do as well as we did; as I said before, there were many good ballplayers in the area. The first few games we played, whether they were close or we clearly dominated our opponent, were always crowd-pleasing ones; before long people looked forward to every game we played. This included the local police, because it was the only time the streets in downtown East End Newport News were quiet. Local drug dealers and want-be pimps were also attending the games. I never realized the revenue that these games helped the Club with.

Pooh Johnson would always let us get first pick at the jerseys when we played. Some players from the other teams would complain. I was starting to wonder about this myself. One day someone from another team asked Mr. Johnson how come Dousey-n-Em always got first pick of the basketball jerseys. He invited the person to look out into the gym just before the game started and asked him to look around; of course, the gym was packed, and people were even standing between the aisles of bleachers. Then he said, "When your team starts packing the gym like that every time they play, I'll start letting you guys have first pick at the jerseys." Although the guy still didn't think this was right and he probably had a good point, he surely got the point Pooh Johnson was making.

Mr. Johnson also found opportunities to give us lessons on life during these games—how to treat people, be generous, and even a lesson in hygiene. Of course, there were signs reminding those who used the lockers and showers to pick up after themselves. Even after Mr. Johnson reminded the teams going in to be mindful about not leaving dirty sportswear on the floor, someone would often leave a used jockstrap on the floor. In between games, Mr. Johnson would go into the locker room for an inspection. If he found someone's underwear or jock on the floor, he would grab a stick about three feet long, lift the item off the floor, and come out into the gym with the bleachers full of spectators, walk toward the two teams who had just played and ask who had left their nasty drawers on the floor. This was like a half-time show to the spectators, but it was really effective. Although he was not able to pinpoint exactly who left those items on the floor, it was embarrassing for the entire team. Several weeks of games would pass before someone would dare to leave something on the floor again.

When We Were Not at the Club

During the summer, outside of sports activities, we would go swimming at the recreation center near Huntington High School. In the Stewart Garden area, there was a recreation center that had a public swimming pool we would go to as well. Our selection of which pool we attended depended on the number of girls at each pool. Building go-carts from about anything you name was something else that kept us out of a lot of trouble during the summer. I remember one of our biggest challenges was to build one without the wheels falling off when we would race down Twenty-Fifth Street Bridge.

Like most inner-city children, we had to build our own bicycles. It wasn't until I was about fifteen years of age that my mother could afford to buy my brother and myself our own bikes. We used to live near the junkyard where we would sneak in at night and steal bicycle parts. We would have gotten the parts from Mr. Turkey Tom, but we didn't want to take the chances of getting shot. This junkyard was owned by some really nice white men. This is the same junkyard where we would sell copper wire after we would steal it from construction sites. One day on a Sunday when the junkyard was closed, we learned—too late—that the owner had decided to put a guard dog inside the compound. We thought that no one even realized that the parts were missing. Two of us would go and hop the fence, while the others would stay outside and watch. The two who would go would be the ones who did not go last time; we used a rotation schedule.

It was my brother's and Todd's turn to go inside the compound this time. Things seemed to be normal at first— until we heard this wicked growl that sent those looking out on the outside running across the street. We then realized that my brother Douglas and Todd were still inside the junkyard. We had started heading back to the compound when we noticed some bike parts coming over the top of the fence. The dog was still growling and started to bark. We then saw Douglas and Todd hopping back over the fence. I can't believe that these guys, while being chased by a dog, still felt it necessary to get the bike parts over the fence. Todd and Douglas received the medal of bravery for stupid valor award. We would give those out for stuff like this. We all had our share of them.

Bicycles were our main source of transportation. We would ride our bikes for miles to the mall and to the waterfront to go fishing and crabbing. We would also venture into some of the other cities that made up the tidewater area. The city of Hampton, which borders Newport News to the east, had drive-in theaters. We would ride our bikes into the exit of the drive-in and grab a speaker off one of the poles in the back of the lot and watch movies for free. I can't believe we never got caught doing this, but something happened where it did come to an end.

One evening while returning home from the drive-in theater, my brother, my cousin Garland, Sandy, and myself were pulled over by the Hampton city police. We just knew it was about sneaking into the drive-in theaters, but it turned out that there was a law in Hampton where it was illegal to ride a bicycle after sundown in the city without a headlight on the bike. We thought we would just get a warning, but we received tickets and had to appear in court. Now I know many of you are probably saying in your mind that the police officer was most likely white. No, he was black. That's why I thought we were going to just get a warning. I didn't really know what to think; he was actually the first black cop I had ever seen in person. The only other one I had seen was Linc Hayes on the *Mod Squad*. Can you believe he actually called for backup? He explained in a nice way why this was necessary. Although this cop was really nice to us, we still labeled him an Uncle Tom and we still had to appear in court.

As I mentioned earlier, I had a few hobbies. I would sometimes build models. At that time a person could mail-order a model car, plane, or boat for just a couple of bucks; this included shipping and handling. It took me about three or four months to save up for one model at a time. This hobby did help a friend get rehabilitated from drugs. We had a lot of glue sniffers in the area, and one was a good friend of mine named Darnell, who later became addicted. This was not because of building models, as some had thought. Although he knew I built these models, he was not interested in the hobby at that time. He just got with the wrong group of guys.

I did not associate with him much after that. He was about twelve when he got started. Within a year after that, he had gotten into so much trouble, he finally ended up in juvenile detention. When he completed his time, his parole officer recommended that he associate with some young people who were trying their best to stay out of trouble. The PO also recommended that he pick up a hobby. My friend mentioned that he had a friend with the hobby of building models. He failed to mention that I used the same glue that glue sniffers used to get high. The PO thought it would be a great idea if he started associating with me again and pick up the same hobby.

To tell you the truth, I really didn't pick up on this at first. As we were gluing the parts together for our first model, I noticed this spaced-out look on his face; it then came back to me that he used to sniff glue to get high. I asked him if building these models would be a problem for him. He said it would not, and that after getting out of juvenile detention, he kept thinking about starting to sniff glue again to get high. He felt that model-building would be the best way to wean himself away for misusing glue. I was starting to second-guess why I really enjoyed building these models so much.

I then asked Darnell what got him started. He said one day a friend much older than he was sitting on the curve near Twenty-Fifth and Jefferson with a brown bag up against his face. The person sniffing the glue asked Darnell if he would like to try it. Darnell refused at first and asked why he sniffed the stuff. His friend told him that after you get high off model glue, a person can see through a girl's clothes. He went on to say that every time he wanted to see a woman naked, he would get high off glue. That's all it took to get Darnell started down the wrong path. I'm glad that I was a little older when hearing this, because he might have gotten me with this one. Darnell did enjoy the hobby and never returned to sniffing glue as a recreational drug habit.

If I did one of my favorite hobbies today, I would be labeled a threat to national security. I would build my own rockets and what I thought was fireworks. Once again, we could not afford to buy our own. I would take books of matches, which were only about 2¢ a pack, scrape the powder off the sticks, and use it for rocket fuel. I had problems with trying to get my rockets to fly straight. They would take off and go in different directions, sometimes causing problems for the neighbors. There was one time when I just knew I had a winner. I placed the fins on the rear of the rocket in what I thought would be best for this rocket to take off and fly straight up. I placed what I thought was the proper weight on the other end. But when I ignited the rocket, it took off on a horizontal flight and zoomed right past a neighbor getting into a car. Of course, you can imagine what was going through his head experiencing this in East End Newport News. I just discreetly snuck back into the house.

One of the most dangerous of all my hobbies was building what I can only call dynamite from match powder. I thought I was making my own firecrackers. I started out rolling up cardboard about the size of a firecracker and pouring the match powder inside. Sometimes they would explode or just take off in any direction like rockets. I then started using my mother's empty medicine bottles. Also, instead of scraping the powder off the matchsticks (paper ones), I started just cutting the heads off the stick rows. I was able to save so much time. I would pour the match heads into the medicine bottle until it was full, then I would take a hot spoke from a bike wheel and poke a hole in the plastic cap of the medicine bottle. Then I would take some match powder and pour it into a sheet of Tops cigarette paper (of course, I had to keep this hidden from my mother). I then rolled a very thin wick and inserted it through the bottle top about halfway. Then I would screw the top on the medicine bottle.

When I first tried this, I had no idea how powerful these things were going to be. Normally when I ignited my own fireworks, I would just stand a few feet away from them.

I learned right away I could not do this with these guys. The first one I tried blew up, and small lit-up match heads went just about everywhere; some of them shot at least forty or fifty feet in the air. I had to turn my back toward the explosion and could feel these match heads on fire fly past me. I couldn't wait to show the fellas. Which I soon learned was a bad idea.

Before guns were as bad as they are today in the inner cities, blank pistols were popular. People used them to scare the snot out of other people. Some of us were able to find these blank rounds in places hidden by our parents or older brothers. My mother did not own a gun, not that I was aware of. She still had some live rounds that were left by my father when he was in the army during the Korean War. We would take some of these live and blank rounds and put them in a hole we would dig about a foot deep and about a foot in diameter. We then would ball up sheets of paper and place them in the hole with the rounds, set the paper on fire, and just stand back and listen to the rounds go off.

On one occasion, we lost count of the number of rounds we placed in the hole compared to the number of bangs we heard. About twenty minutes after the fire went out, we felt that it would be safe to approach the hole. Todd decided he would go confirm this. When he looked over into the hole, we all heard another pop! Todd grabbed his belly and started running back toward us. We all thought that he was joking around, which he was known for doing. As he got closer to us, I noticed that he had blood coming through his fingers. We were hoping that it wasn't one of the live rounds, but what else could it have been? I asked him to move his hand away so I could see the wound. It turned out that the back shell from one of the blanks had lodged into the surface of his abdomen. I was able to pull it away. The worst part of this experience was what took place after Todd lied about it to his mother and she found out what really happened. We all at the time wished we had gotten shot by the live rounds.

By the time I was fifteen, most of the other attractions and recreation outside of the Club were being torn down or closed up. There were three main theaters: the Jefferson, the Dixie, and the Moton. The Moton is still standing to this day, but not as a movie theater. There were some teenage hangouts or nonalcoholic clubs that were popular, like the Black Lite and the Teenage Hop. The Armory, the YWCA, and other recreational faculties had parties and dances. And what city didn't have its block parties? Every time one of these places were closed or torn down, the membership at the Club would increase.

Young girls were starting to become envious of the young boys having a place to go when they didn't. The YWCA was in the northern part of Newport News and did not offer as many attractions as HRBC. Although the Peninsula Boys and Girls Club today would make the cut, it was called the Peninsula Boys Club then; it did not offer as much as HRBC, and the facility was much smaller. But any recreation facility that helped keep any youths off the street and out of trouble needed to be commended for their efforts, even if it only had one basketball goal.

The directors of HRBC were starting to think of ways to include girls as members. Of course, we had mixed feelings about it. We welcomed the girls to come and watch us do what we thought "man things," but we did not want them to participate, except during dances, skating, and the annual penny carnival. But, of course, this was soon to change.

HARD TIMES

The anxieties from growing up in hard times really manifest themselves for a young person the most when attending school. Only those who have similar backgrounds can really understand why a person would be ready to drop out of school because of not having the latest designer clothes or shoes. Today as I reflect on this part of my past, I can't believe I let this type of peer pressure keep me from attaining the level of education that I had available to me like everyone else. When I say level of education, I mean the most a young person can achieve in high school, with the advanced and accelerated classes available then.

My mother did her best to relieve her children of these anxieties. She understood how mean kids could be in school, but she had no idea how tough it had gotten. She had that sticks-and-stones-may-break-my-bones-but-names-can-never-hurt-you attitude. Little did she know that name-calling by this time was getting young people killed—even when you did the best you could to avoid a fight. Unfortunately she could only afford to help my older sister most of the time. My younger brother and I had to accept whatever was left and just deal with the pressure from our peers head-on.

It's good to see that many schools today have mandatory school uniforms. Anyone reading this book experiencing similar anxieties, please do not give up. Take advantage of the education that's available to you.

Holiday celebrations brought on more anxieties for me and my family than anything else. There were times my dad would go out and find a tree that someone was throwing away because they had bought a new one. Not to mention those toys for tots my mom used to get us. I started to realize that if we asked my mother for just one good gift, this would make it easier for her and we had a better chance of getting what we wanted. I don't care what people say: if you're not in a position to afford these celebrations, it can cause shame and a lot pain and embarrassment for an individual and a family. I always wondered why God would have people celebrate something only people who have money can enjoy.

I remember when I was in the sixth or seventh grade and Christmas was only a few weeks away. They had us pull names to see who we would buy a gift for. I wanted to skip class that day because I knew I did not have the money to buy anybody a gift. Well, I decided to go anyways. I was really hoping that I would pick one of my homeys' names. If I did, I would have just punched them in the arm and said "Merry Christmas." But can you believe I ended up picking the name of a white girl in the class? I didn't have a clue what to buy her. I certainly wasn't going to ask her. I went and told my mother that I needed to get a gift for a classmate and that we had to bring it to class next week before the Christmas break. She kindly said no, and then she emphatically said no, then she said no in other ways to help me understand not to ask her again. I tried doing some of my door-to-door hustling, like asking people if they needed something from the store. I earned about five cents to a quarter for each trip. It's amazing how things get tight around this time of the year. No one was interested in paying someone to go to the store.

My mother started to feel sorry for me. She said that if she had the money, she would help me out. I decided to ask my dad; but before I had a chance to ask him, he asked me what I was going to get him for Christmas. Oh, he was serious. Time was running out. I just decided I would not go to school on that day. I felt so much better. A few days before we had to bring our gifts in, my mother asked me to go to the grocery store with her to buy food. She only had food stamps. While we were in the store, I saw a box of Life-Savers candy that was already wrapped up for this occasion. It had about eight rows of the candy in different flavors, four on each side, and it opened up like a book to display the different flavors. I grabbed it and took it to my mother and asked if she could please buy it for me so I would have a gift to give in school. She said that I should be glad that she could pay for it using the food stamps.

When the time came for me to give the gift, I wasn't sure how the girl would receive it. You should have seen the look on her face when I gave it to her! She was so happy about the gift, and all the other kids were envious about the gift she received. Just when I was about to feel real good about what I gave her, one of the girls from my neighborhood yelled out, " We all know you used food stamps to buy it!" What made things even worse, the person who was supposed to bring me a gift didn't come to class that day.

Some think that financial assistance (welfare) is a waste of taxpayers' money, but let me tell you about some statistics in the inner city and urban areas that may change most people's minds. True, there are many people who abused welfare and continue to do so. Of course, there have been some improvements made in managing the system. One thing that I do know is that there are some youths growing up in the urban setting that, had it not been for these government programs, they would have been counted among those who choose to be a problem in society no matter where they may be living or their financial situation. If these programs did not exist, I would have found a way to survive. Just think: five out of twenty young men growing up in the hood may escape jail time and go on to become a great asset to society as long as their parents—or parent, which was the case most of the time—receive some type of assistance from the government. But take this away, and taxpayers would have to most likely try to rehabilitate all twenty instead of fifteen.

THE DOZENS

Everyone in an urban area understood what the dozens meant. It was something that most people believe is very innocent. It certainly could be, depending on who was involved. But what most people don't understand is that the person who usually talked about your mother was a very close friend that would probably hurt anyone else who would say the same thing about your mother. I had a lot of Eddie Haskell-type friends, you know, the guy from *Leave It to Beaver*. He would have so much respect for Beaver's mom in her presence and was completely different when he was not. The guys in my neighborhood were ten times worse. In the presence of your mother, they would give her all the respect in the world, even doing things for her that I didn't want to do, but they were ruthless with words in other places. But it was all understood.

It's amazing what you can get away with saying about someone's mother, but it can be very serious if you say something that directly criticizes the person. I learned this lesson early in life. One day I was at the Club watching some other team play before we played. During the game a guy I knew in the neighborhood decided he would talk about my mom and everyone else in my family. This guy was really good. I mean, he had everybody in a five-foot radius of us cracking up. It got to the point where those who could hear him were no longer interested in the game. Others who were not sitting close by came over to see why everyone was laughing so hard. He just kept going at it. I did not say anything back to him. I did have some pretty good yo' mama jokes, but this guy knew how poor I was and I did not stand a chance.

I was just hoping that he would soon get tired of picking on me and turn his attention to someone else. It certainly didn't seem like he was going to run out of things to say. There were even some young girls there my age whom I had a crush on that heard what he was saying and laughed as well. Some started to feel sorry for me and began asking him to leave me alone. He then said he would give me a break because it looked like I was about to start crying. My eyes were starting to tear up, but I denied that I was about to cry. He then came about six inches from my face yelling, "You know you want to start crying!" I just kept shaking my head, assuring him I was not about to cry. He then got even closer in to my face and kept asking me, "Why do you have tears in your eyes?" I looked him in the eyes and said, "Because your breath smells like onions."

All of a sudden, everyone who heard him talking about my mother became quiet for about three seconds, and then there was an outburst of laughs that you could hear outside the gym. He looked at me, smiled for about a second, then started swinging at me; those who were close by immediately tried to break it up. When Pooh Johnson came over to see what was going on, he asked both of us to leave the gym. Everyone assured Pooh that the other guy started the fight from the beginning. I did not want to leave because we were going to play the next game. Pooh Johnson saw how much older and larger this guy was compared to me and knew he would have killed me outside the gym. He also knew that I never really started any fights in the Club.

He then just asked the other guy to leave and said I could stay. If Al and Bobby were there, it would have been a real mess. I was hoping they would show up later, because this guy might decide he was going to wait until I left the gym. I was expecting Bobby because he played on the same team as I. Al and Bobby did show up, but the guy did not hang around till after the game. I really believe if I had just said something about his mother instead, there would not have been a confrontation.

Racism in East End?

Racism is usually straightforward in an inner-city area. It wasn't any different in East End Newport News. White people didn't like blacks, and blacks didn't trust white people. This is what a person growing up in the area was taught to believe. "Everything's sblibby" was the phrase of the day. Meaning everything was black. This was certainly a true statement because no whites lived in the area. It was definitely a change for my sister, brother, and me. In New Haven, everybody was just everybody. The neighborhood was very diverse. The only time race became a issue for someone my age was when Martin Luther King was assassinated and James Brown came out with the hit "Say It Loud—I'm Black and I'm Proud." Most of us in the neighborhood really didn't know what to do or think about the talk of racial prejudice.

I really was confused when the Black Panthers in the area were going through the neighborhood reaching out to young black children. What was ironic for my brother and me was when he and I were walking a few blocks to visit some friends and two members tried to talk to us about racism, inviting us to some of the functions they set up for young blacks. They were white. At least we thought they were. It was a man and woman; both had blond hair and blue eyes. They both wore black berets and leather jackets. The man had a curly blond Afro, and the woman's blond hair was straight. They actually looked like hippies with Black Panther garb. People to this day still have a hard time believing this when I tell them about the experience. Especially those in all-black neighborhoods at that time. They tell me that they were not black but just two high yellow people. I'm pretty much sure to this day that they were indeed white.

Whether it was intentional or not, the goal in Dickerson Court was to convince you that a black person could not in any way trust white people. Although I experienced some things in the public schools, especially after busing was enforced in Newport News, that helped me see why they might want to believe this, I just had a hard time accepting it. This was because I lived in an ethnically diverse area before. It was also because of our New England accent and the fact that my brother, sister, and I at the time were familiar only with the black music artists that my parents listened to, like the Temptations, Otis Redding, and Aretha Franklin. But we also listened to Elton John, Alice Cooper, and other white artists, which we were teased a lot for. Thanks are due to our friend Sandy, who introduced us to music by Earth, Wind & Fire and Sly Stone. Todd introduced me to Funk music by Parliament Funkadelic. My brother got a Commodores album from Al and Bobby. I could not believe how this type of music got past us. The conversion did not take long; we fell in love with the music. We were starting to listen to radio stations with black disc jockeys only. Although we were now hip to R&B music, my sister and I would still occasionally turn to another radio station when we needed a soft rock fix. I'm glad we caught on.

When I was in the tenth grade, some of the older youths in the neighborhood who played in the band at school would make it a point to rush to the back of the bus, even to the point of going through the emergency exit in the back. They did this in order to play some funky tones while riding to school. It was always amusing to see another bus pull up beside ours and see a bunch of Afros and braids bobbing their heads to the funky beat. Even though the bus driver hated it when they did this, there were times you would catch him tapping his feet and bobbing his head.

The notion that you just can't trust white people still was not setting well with me. There were some whites who would come and visit in the neighborhood, and some would even venture out to some of the soul-food restaurants on Jefferson Avenue. There's no way in the world these individuals would risk their lives to come to this part of town to get some good-tasting greasy-spoon food that is sure to clog the arteries if they had a problem with blacks. Yet this feeling of distrust was very strong in the neighborhood.

When people starting talking about Jesus not being white but being a man of color, some could not understand why it was hard for some blacks in the area to accept this. From what I experienced in the neighborhood, it wasn't because blacks had been brainwashed for so long into believing this or that they hated themselves; it was because Jesus for a lot of blacks was the only white man they trusted. You would often hear someone say, "The only white man I trust is Jesus." The others that some might have trusted if they were living would have been the Kennedy brothers. There were pictures of John Kennedy, Bobby Kennedy, and Martin Luther King Jr. all together that were popular in the area. My mom had one hanging on the wall.

By the time I graduated from high school and heard talk about the ills of racism, I thought they were talking about us having the problem. Even under these conditions, I never felt I had a problem with race. It was about a year after I had been discharged from the army that one day I decided to go over to the gym to play some basketball. Normally the courts at this gym were full, but when I got there, it was only one person on the court playing. This individual was white. As I watched him, he seemed to have a pretty decent game. He was about an inch taller than I was. I asked if I could shoot around with him on the court. He said "sure." After about twenty minutes, I decided to ask if he wanted to play one-on-one. Again he said "sure."

I let him take the ball out first because I felt I was going to win anyways. I don't know if he was trying to hustle me, but his game seemed to be a lot better than what it was when we was just shooting around. I then started to step mine up a little. By this time he was up four or five points. I then started to play my best, and the game got pretty intense. I mean, we continued to show good sportsman-like conduct toward each other, but anyone watching the game could tell that we were taking the game pretty serious.

I was able to catch up and tie the game. For the next twenty minutes, we just kept denying each other the final basket. Then he did something I thought was impossible. I was just barely five feet eleven inches tall. I could dunk the ball if I got a good running start. Now as I mentioned earlier, this guy was only about an inch taller than I. We, of course, were following the take-the-ball-back rule when the shooter missed a shot. This rule did not apply to the one shooting the ball. He tried to shoot a ten footer, and I just put my hand up to block the shot. The ball bounced off the rim. And just when I was about to jump for the rebound, this guy leaped over me and slam-dunked the ball. I could not believe it! I went on to tell him that was a good dunk and I really enjoyed playing with him.

Before this game, I never got upset about losing a game, and this was not the first time someone dunked in my face. I played in an intramural league when I was stationed in Germany. But this was the first time someone white did it. So I just went home and took a shower. The minute I left the gym and for the next couple of days, I was really upset. At the time I could not understand why I was having a hard time accepting losing to this guy. I then started to take an honest look into my heart and realized that if he was black, I would have forgotten about the game by now. I finally realized that my background had a negative effect on me when it came to other races of people. If it had not been for this game and having taken an honest look at myself, I would have continued to believe that I didn't have a problem. It may be a long ways from a seriously racist person, but what little was there needed to be adjusted.

Lesson learned for me. When it comes to race, I think we all really need to take a careful and honest look at ourselves before we even think about trying to correct others about their attitudes toward other races.

First Football Season

Todd was the only one on my block that was seriously thinking about trying out. I was twelve years old at this time. I did want to play, but I was just plain scared because of the older boys I heard were trying out for the team; most of them had played the previous year or two. Todd and I went to the first day of practice. It looked like a hundred people were trying out. The Club normally had an intramural league and had several teams that would play each other. Newport News had a city league, which finally allowed HRBC to join. This year was the first year HRBC played in the city league.

Each time Todd came to pick me up to go to practice, I would get very nervous. I couldn't understand why, because when we played sandlot tackle football with no equipment, I did pretty good. Todd did not seem to have any anxieties about playing with these older guys with more experience in organized football. Each time we went to practice, we would go through the drills but football equipment was limited. You see, none of us could afford to buy our own. The clubs supplied the equipment. Veteran players would get first pick. The coach would say each week that some would not return, and those young rookies like us would eventually get helmets and shoulder pads as long as we didn't give up. Todd's older brother gave him a helmet that he used in high school. This thing weighed a ton. But it was a very nice helmet, so each practice day we would just walk down to the field with that one helmet between us, feeling real good about ourselves and telling people we played on the team when asked.

At the start of the summer, we decided to build a clubhouse in a field where we normally played sandlot tackle football. Across the street from where we lived, some new apartments for low-income families were being constructed. We would take wood and nails that the construction guys were no longer using to build the clubhouse. From watching them, we got a good idea how to start with the frame and then the sidings. Well, one day while working on the clubhouse, I stepped on a nail; about a half inch went into the bottom of my foot right through my tennis shoe. I had to get a tetanus shot. I could have continued to play football, but I used this as an excuse to stop going to practice. The real reason for not going was the larger and older boys playing, and I was very thin for my age. Football was after all a contact sport, so I was terrified of getting hit (tackled).

Todd continued to go. I would see him leave each day with that one helmet and not come back with anything else. I would always ask him when he was going to get the shoulder pads, jersey, and pants. He would just say that more people were not coming to practice, and it was just a matter of time. I then asked him when the first game was, and he said in about two weeks. I said to myself, *poor Todd is going to be sitting on that bench with just that one helmet and nothing else.* I started to feel better about not going to practice.

Well, on game day, something happened that helped me appreciate why we should not give up if we are determined to do something. I was standing in front of my door when I saw Todd in full uniform. The helmet his brother gave him was painted blue with a white stripe down the center; it looked really nice. He had a dark blue jersey, shoulder pads, and white pants with blue stripes down the side. It was the same style and colors as the Baltimore Colts uniform. I could not believe my eyes.

THE NEXT YEAR

This time I was determined to make the football team, especially after hearing that Dousey, who was younger, had made the team last year. But trying out for the team this year was very challenging for me. For some reason there weren't many rookies trying out. I just knew I was going to be riding the bench for the first year. I was one of the smallest boys out there. Most of the guys I knew had already played at least one year. And they seemed to be pretty good. There were a few things the coach always made clear to us, and one was that size does not make a ballplayer—and if you get cut from the team, it's only because you decided not to come back. Basically if you get cut, it's only because you cut yourself.

Since most of us came from poor families, the Club provided the uniforms and the equipment. They had plenty of good shoulder pads and helmets. You had to buy your own cleats (turf shoes). Before the Club was allowed to play in the city league, they had their own intramural football league. Before the Club, there were no all-black recreation teams in the city league. And there was only maybe one team in the league that had maybe one or two black players. The coach would let all the veteran players choose their equipment first. Although there was plenty of good equipment, the Club also had its share of some very old and beat-up stuff. So by the time the veteran players finished picking though the goods, the rest of us had to pick from what was left.

The coach would have us line up and race to the equipment after blowing the whistle three times. First, with all the veteran players, then with the rookies. If I didn't have anything else going for me, I did have speed. I really can't remember anyone on the team who could beat me in the fifty-yard dash. So I knew that I would have a better chance at picking some decent equipment from what was left over. When the coach blew his whistle for the third time, I know I reached the pile of equipment two to three seconds before everyone else. But as I approached the equipment, I almost started to cry and leave. I can't begin to describe how old some of the helmets and shoulder pads were. It looked like some of the stuff was left over from the fifties. I was just able to grab the best of what was left.

Some of the other guys said "no way; I will save up my money and buy my own." They called what was left "suicide equipment." Someone said they saw a helmet without the faceguard in the pile. My shoulder pads had tube socks tied around and between the upper and lower shoulder pad on each side. None of the knee, hip, and thigh pads for the pants matched. As we were walking back toward the veteran players, they had a field day with jokes about the equipment we had. Now I could see why Todd during his first tryout year went to practice wearing only that one helmet he got from his older brother.

I decided that I would not put on what I had until I arrived at practice. The defense coach told us not to worry, and as long as we continued to come back, better equipment would be available. Because others, believe it or not, like the veteran players would not come back. They would send the equipment back via other players. I knew I had no other choice but to wait.

I now had to start focusing on how to get a pair of turf shoes to play in. Our first scrimmage game was against a visiting club. It was a control scrimmage. I was on the sidelines just watching the game and was very nervous. That was one of the reasons I was hoping that the coaches would not ask me to play. The other was because by this time I was the only one left with the ancient equipment and practice uniform. The other rookies had either bought their own equipment or just quit. I knew the coaches were anxious to see me play, because I was doing so well during practice.

Then I heard the defense coach say, "Sam! Where are you? It's time to see some action." As soon as I ran out on the field, some of the spectators started laughing. I was so embarrassed. But the thing that really ticked me off was when the other team started making fun of what I had on. Since I was the smallest guy out there, the defense coach had already warned me that they would be coming my way. I was, believe it or not, playing defensive end. As the coach said they would, the next play came directly at me. I hit the running back so hard, my pants came down. Everyone on the sidelines started cheering but still making fun of my equipment and uniform. The other team just kept sending plays my way, and I kept shutting them down. By this time, the spectators were cheering for me without the jokes, and the other team started to take me seriously. I had to earn this same respect from my own teammates. After that game, I started in every game.

My first game experience of the regular season was exciting but embarrassing. Our first game was against one of the toughest teams in the league, Sanford, which we suffered a humiliating loss to. Actually we lost every game.

We did get one win from a forfeit (the other team did not show up). Of course, it was hard when returning to the neighborhood to hear someone ask that infamous question, "Did yawl win?" It got to the point where they stopped asking did we win, but how much did we lose by. As for me, I didn't pay too much attention to the question or about losing. I was just glad to be in a football uniform and able to play and return home with some grass stains and dirt on my clothes. It was really depressing if you lost and returned home squeaky clean.

Every game I would take notes on how to improve. I would also watch some of the veteran players' every move. We had a middle linebacker nicknamed Barboy, who was fearless on defense and well-known in the city league. Dousey also was an exceptional player and would give me pointers on how to tackle without getting hurt. Most of the sandlot tackle moves I learned from playing in the neighborhood could get you killed. We had several guys on the team with interesting nicknames—Dousey, Barboy, Sput, Blowpop, and Rock.

I remember when we played Deer Park. I was very nervous about this game because everyone was talking about the star quarterback they had. On one play in the first quarter, he decided to bootleg to the left, which was away from me; because the left side was shut down, he decided to come back in the other direction toward me. I was trying to square my shoulder up against his midsection, but my entire helmet went directly into his abdomen and he was laid out. He then had to leave the game, which made it a very close one. We still lost. I received a lot of "that's what I'm talking about" and daps (low fives), but my neck was killing me.

A Winning Season

After a humiliating first season, you can imagine all the anxieties that we all were facing starting the next. I was now more comfortable and confident about participating in organized sports. I had experience under my belt. I had taken very careful notes about the technique of the game, and most of all, I had learned to deal with my complex about being so small. I was really looking forward to this year's tryouts and the regular season games. Although most of us veterans in the game may have believed that our starting position was locked in, there was always a slight fear about some rookie or someone coming from another league with more experience that would snatch it right from under you. I noticed that over the summer most of the guys gained a lot of weight. Some seemed like they grew five to six inches in three months. It's a good thing that there was a weight limit.

As for me, I think the only thing that grew was my confidence in the game. I never thought I was better than anyone else, just good enough to start, if that makes any sense. The weigh-in for this year brought on a lot of anxieties as well. For most of us, this was going to be our last season because of age and weight. Age fifteen was the maximum age limit, and you had to turn fifteen after July 31. But the maximum weight was 135 pounds. Most of us second- and third-year veterans were aged thirteen to fifteen. The problem was that just about every boy age fourteen and fifteen was a few pounds over the weight requirement. The goal was to get all overweights below the weight limit before the weigh-in.

I was one of the oldest but smallest players on the team. Even Dousey at age thirteen had me by five or ten pounds, and he looked small to me. I can't imagine how I looked to him. But the most embarrassing thing for me was the day of the weigh-in. Everyone who approached the scale was asked to take their clothes off to be sure they met the weight requirement. Some had to get on the scale completely nude to make the weigh-in. When I walked up to the scale, I was about to take my clothes off, but the person taking our weight looked at me and said not to bother taking my clothes off. I asked him, "What about my shoes?" He just looked at me and said, "Just get on the scale."

Most of the guys on the team were envying me because I didn't have to take anything off, but I felt really embarrassed. Here I was one of the oldest players on the team. Todd was the only guy older than me, but yet the youngest on the team wasn't asked to keep his clothes on. I could see it if we were horse jockeys, but this was football. There were some who kind of snickered about it when I had my back turned. It wasn't that I was short for my age but just very skinny, so I started thinking that maybe keeping my clothes on would be better. I can just imagine some of the comments that would have been made if the guys saw me looking like J. J. from *Good Times*.

There were a couple players who had to return for a makeup weigh-in. One was our star middle linebacker

Barboy, who was a key player and the team's defense captain. After everyone was dressed, any embarrassing moments during the weigh-in were soon forgotten and we started to focus mainly on playing football. Those who needed to return for the makeup weigh-in did meet the weight requirement the second time.

Like the year before, there was a lot of talk about all the players in the league who we should be scared to death of. Our peers talked about these guys like these individuals should be playing pro football instead of Little League. One of the players everyone was talking about was the son of my last year gym coach, who I did not like very much. At the middle school I attended, it was okay for the gym coach to spank you with a paddle if you did not participate in any of the physical exercises. At the start of the year, my mother could not yet afford to pay my gym fee, which covered your gym uniform (a T-shirt, gym shorts, and a pair of socks); you also got a pair of jockstraps. The fee also paid for the towels and washcloths you needed to take a shower with. By the way, it was also okay for the gym coach to spank you if you did not take a shower. The coach would do this with just your gym shorts and your jockstrap on; it was mandatory to wear your shorts and jockstrap during PE.

Health class and gym were mandatory. If you took health the first semester, then you took gym the second; if you took gym first, you took health the second semester. I tried to take my health class the first semester and then gym during the second. This would allow my mother time to save up for my gym fee. I was always told that rules were made to be broken. That was not the case in this school. Plus I was too ashamed to mention to anyone why I would like to take the health class first. I had all these excuses why I could not participate in the physical exercises.

One day the gym coach finally got tired of all my excuses and decided I should get paddled. I decided then to tell him that I just could not afford the price of the gym fee. He did not want to hear any more excuses. Maybe I should have told him this at first. The coach was a short stocky guy that looked like a boulder with muscles. Everyone feared getting paddled by this guy. Those who were paddled would go into his office, and you could hear them getting paddled clear outside the gymnasium. I said there was no way I would let this guy paddle me. No, I did not do the same thing to him as I did to my fourth-grade teacher. I decided I would just go to the principal's office and talk to him about it. Although the principal probably would have done the same thing, at least he didn't look like the Incredible Hulk.

As I started walking away from the coach, he had three guys in the next higher grade and older wrestle me back to his office. At first I could not understand why he thought it would take three guys older and so much larger than I to strong-arm me to his office. He must have seen the fear in my eyes. I really gave these guys a hard time getting me back to his office. The guys kept telling me to stop being a punk and take the lick like a man. One of the guys, who later became a good friend, said, "Sam, just go ahead and get it over with; it's just one pop, and it will be over."

I decided then to stop resisting and do as he suggested. When the coach pulled out this large paddle with holes in it, I tried everything I could to not look like I was afraid. He then asked me, "Do you know why the holes are in the paddle?" Before I had a chance to answer, he started swinging the paddle (doing practice swings) and said it helped keep the resistance down when swinging the paddle. By this time, fear had turned into anger. I just looked at him like if I could, I would make him eat that paddle for lunch. He then asked me to bend over and touch my toes. As I was thinking about all the different ways I would get revenge against the coach and the students he used to muscle me in the office, I heard a loud pop. Immediately after, I felt a stinging sensation like I never felt before in my life. It started to burn pretty bad. I stood up and just smiled at everyone with watery eyes. Of course, I said to myself that I would one day get these guys back. I just decided to skip gym until my mother was able to afford to pay the gym fee.

When I found out that the coach's son played for Parkview, I could not wait to play these guys. Everyone who had seen him practice said he was a short muscular stump like his dad who would just completely run over people. All during the practice season, I heard about this guy—and just when I was about to become concerned about it, I remembered that day when his dad paddled me. It was a different type of anxiety for me when thinking about playing Parkview. We played them the second game of the season. Both teams had won the first game, which was a major accomplishment for us. When that day came, I was really what they call pumped up.

When we got on the bus for the game, we would start with our club chants. Dousey would take the lead in getting us started. I don't care what age you are when playing organized sports, you have to agree that these chants helped you prepare mentally for the game. Our best and simplest chant was just shouting, "Giants! Giants! Giants!"

When we arrived at the field as the visiting team, I just kept trying to find the gym coach's son. When I looked over at their sideline, I noticed that my last year's gym coach was there on the sideline to support his son. I finally had a chance to see his son. He looked just like everyone said and the way I imagined he would. Short and muscular like his father, with thick thighs. A little fear of what this guy might do to me when I got a chance to tackle him started to surface. Revenge! Not that I'm encouraging this, but I was just fourteen years old. This was just great! Plus I knew the first play was coming around my end. And sure enough it did.

The quarterback pitched the ball to my old gym coach's son as he came running around the left side, and to me he looked like he could run through a wall. I was able to get past his blockers, and he and I squared up right at the scrimmage line. He actually tried to run right over me. He lowered his shoulder to gain more leverage, but I just leveled my left shoulder pad right below his belt and stood him up. We came at each other running full speed. He weighed a good twenty-five or thirty pounds more than I did. He looked like he was twice my size in width. The impact was so loud that people on the sidelines gasped in unison.

I thought that I would be the one going backward; but to my surprise, forward momentum was on my side, and he was the one landing on his back. About three seconds after the hit and everyone's gasping, it became quiet. He then pushed me off top of him, and when I stood up, I looked him right in his eyes. He hopped up and said he would be coming back this way. I told him I'd be here waiting for him. I turned to my teammates, who were really beside themselves. I thought they were never going to stop hitting my helmet and shoulder pads. I then looked over to the sidelines at the coaches and the rest of my teammates, and the spectators on that side were going crazy. The smallest guy on the team had just leveled one of the most feared running backs in the league. I couldn't wait for the next play to see if he was going to come my way again.

I do have to say that he was a boy of his word, because their next play was an exact repeat of the first. This time the impact was more violent and louder than the first. I was waiting for him to push me off of him; but as I got up, I noticed he was just lying there moving his body from side to side. I then realized that I had knocked the wind out of him. By this time the assistant coaches came on the field to see if he was okay. The referees then called a time-out. When he finally was able to stand and walk off the field, I wanted to say, "I'll be here waiting for your return." I decided to just keep my mouth shut, because the coach had serious issues with unsportsmanlike conduct from his players. But I did walk past his father who was on the sidelines and stared him in his face, hoping he would remember the time he paddled me in gym class.

At this time everyone who was cheering for the Club was going nuts. But as I was walking back to get in the huddle, I noticed that my right shoulder felt a little strange. It had a sort of numb feeling to it. I continued to play the next down, but I started to realize that something was really going on with my shoulder. I then asked the coach to take me out of the game. When I got to the sidelines and explained to them what I was experiencing, they removed my jersey and shoulder pads. That's when they noticed that my shoulder was dislocated. One of the defense coaches just grabbed my shoulder and snapped it back in place. Right away, I started to feel the pain. He asked me how I was feeling, and I asked him to please let me continue to play. I was not finished with the running back or anyone else who planned to run the ball my way. He was okay with me playing if I didn't feel any pain. Of course, I lied and said I was fine.

It really didn't make a difference, because for the rest of the game, not one single play came around my end. Their star running back was back in the game and was doing okay, but the rest of my teammates, especially Barboy, Dousey, and Bobby, kept him from gaining a lot of yards rushing. We basically shut down the running game. They then went to a passing game. Unfortunately for us, they won the game with the score being 6 to 0. We had two of our touchdowns called back for penalties.

We went on to win our next game, which was the third game in the season. Our fourth game was against Fort Eustis, and we played these guys really well. As with Parkview, we pretty much shut down their running game. By halftime we were up 7 to 0. After the half, they came back on the field and started to do something I had never seen before in Little League football—kicking long field goals. They had a little guy who looked no bigger than I kicking thirty- or thirty-five-yard field goals. They ended up winning the game 18 to 14 just by kicking field goals. We had never really practiced for this kind of offense. Usually our coaches would have heard about this guy, but now we were two wins and two losses.

At the next practice, our coaches decided to do something that scared the daylights out of me. They thought that some changes needed to be made on defense. I was hoping that I would not lose my starting position. Both defense coaches had decided to walk to each position on the field and call out the name of the person who would play that position. They then wanted the player to walk and stand in that position. They started with the defensive line first. Anxieties were running high among us, and you could clearly see that on our faces. They started on the opposite side of the end where I was playing. This was the position Bobby was playing. They decided to put someone else in his position. As Bobby's head just bent down, my heart was starting to beat faster. Bobby still had a starting position on offense. When they got to the other defensive end position where I played, they put Bobby in that position. By then I was about ready to cry, which was something I just didn't believe in. Then they started to call names to fill the defensive backs positions. They started again on the opposite side from the side I used to play. The outside linebacker and middle linebacker positions were filled by the same people, except for the cornerback position, which was played by Dousey. When he saw that they put someone else in his position, he just could not believe it; but like a few others on the team, Dousey started on both sides. At this point, I was about to go home.

There were only two positions left, the other outside linebacker position and the other cornerback position. They then called Dousey's name to fill the other cornerback position, so they just switched him over to the other side in the same position. I looked around and saw that there were three of us who had started on defense before and had not yet been called for this last and one of the most wanted positions on the field. The only thing going through my mind was that I was going to be riding the pine as we call it. As everyone just stood on the field wondering who was going to fill this last spot, the coaches were sort of in a huddle having a discussion about what we thought was that last position. They then came out of the huddle and said, "This will be the new starting lineup."

But then someone asked, "What about the right outside linebacker position?" One of the defense coaches just looked down at his clipboard; you could tell by the look on his face that he thought he had already called the name out for this position. Then he said with a loud but familiar tone in his voice, "Sam! Where's Sam?" By this time I was sitting on one knee. When I heard my name, I said, "Here I am, Coach." He responded, "Get over here; you will now be playing in this position."

I can't explain the relief that came upon me that day. This change in the defensive lineup proved to be a very good decision on the coach's part. From that day forward, we became one of the most talked-about defenses in the league.

Like our basketball team, people started to call the football team Dousey-n-Em.

THE BIG GAME

We all were excited about seeing how the new defense arrangement was going to work out. Our next games were Deer Park, Denbigh, South Morrison, and World War II Recreation, which was another all African-American team that was allowed to enter the city league. WWII was to me the toughest team we played and defeated. They had some really good players on the team. They also had some very young coaches and were just out-coached hands down. They clearly saw where our team's strengths were, but for some reason they decided to ignore this and run at us head-on. They were either trying to break the strongest part of the defense down, or it was just plain old pride that got in the way.

To tell the truth, I was glad when that game was over. Although I was hitting pretty hard that game, I was taking a serious beating at the same time. Our star running back Everret, who usually had very little problem running over most of our opponents, was also glad the game was finally over and was hoping that we would not have to play them again that season. But the game we were all looking forward to was Sanford, which had never lost a game in the city league. Sanford usually had all-white players on their team. I just could not forget when we played the year before when they utterly embarrassed us. They had one player who was huge, and he played what seemed like every position on the field. This guy when kicking off to us ran directly at me and knocked me what I thought was about twenty yards backward. I didn't think I was ever going to stop rolling.

This year the head coach decided he would try something different. For years he knew that one of the strategies Sanford used to defeat their opponents was psychological. They would warm up with their larger guys in front, and their warm-up drills were so impressive that anyone watching would be terrified just from this. On game day the coach said he would keep us on the bus until they were finished, and then we could get off the bus just before kickoff and perform our warm-up drill. He also put the larger players in front facing them. We already had an impressive warm-up drill, especially our psych drill in which Dousey always took the lead. But in the meantime, while Sanford was warming up on the field, the coach had us rocking the bus off on the side of the field where we could not see them but they could surely hear us. The chanting of "Giants! Giants! Giants!" sounded like it could be heard miles away.

When Sanford finished their team warm-up drill, the coach told us it was time for us to go out on the field. The team captains, Dousey, Sput, and Barboy, had us so fired up, I thought we were going to lose our minds out there. I saw a look in some of the other players' eyes like I had never seen before. We certainly were mentally ready for it, and we had trained so hard during practice preparing to play a perfect game. This was the reputation Sanford had—a team that made few mistakes and was very disciplined. Since the start of the season, all we heard from the people in the neighborhood was, "I don't care if you guys don't beat anyone else this year; just please beat Sanford." This we also heard from those guys who played on the team before and those who played for the Club before they were allowed to play in the city league. At first the issue seemed to be about race, but it started to mean more than that to us. Defeating Sanford would prove that these inner-city boys were good enough to play on that level.

When we left the bus and got on the field, family members and friends clearly saw a different spirit in us and that we were certainly up for the game. The warm-up drill was flawless. HRBC Giants was ready. I could always tell by the look on the coaches' faces whether they thought we would really win a game or not. Of course, they did their best to hide it, but most of us on the team could tell. This time the coaches had a very positive look on their faces. This was the last and most important thing I needed to see. On the other side of the field, it was not easy to tell if the silence was just fear of maybe losing the game or wondering if they might need police protection.

Sanford had won the coin toss and elected to receive the ball. After we kicked the ball off to them, they were able to get across midfield during the return. Of course, many of us were hoping that we were not ready to cave in from this and that it would not be a repeat of last year. It was just too early in the game, as our coaches and team captains kept assuring us. As always, the next play was a quarterback keeper around the right side toward Bobby, Dousey, and me. We were able to tackle the quarterback behind the line of scrimmage. After that play, it was all HRBC Giants throughout the rest of the game. All of us played better than we had ever played during any game in the season. The right side of our defense looked very small in size, and Sanford just kept coming right at us. Bobby, Dousey, and I were having a field day with tackles. Every time we made a tackle, the spectators on the sidelines went crazy.

The offense played just about a perfect game. Between our quarterback and running backs, we scored three touchdowns. We ended up shutting down Sanford, not allowing them to score any points. After the game, no one could believe we actually beat Sanford. This was the talk of East End Newport News for years. Afterward, many individuals brought their children from other areas of Hampton Roads to join the HRBC. Some are star athletes to this day.

The Second Basketball Season
(The Warm-Ups)

The next basketball season we moved up to the intermediate level, and once again Dousey-n-Em was the team to see at the Club. This was our last season together as a basketball team. We were still high in the clouds from defeating Sanford. Dousey was going to try out for the Newport News Middle School team as well. We were afraid that if he made the team, he would no longer be interested in playing for the Club. Because he was a very good player, we knew he would make the team. And we also knew that if he did, we would not be able to win the play-offs without him.

As we were getting ready and practicing for our last and final season together, Dousey decided that it would be a good idea if we could play the last season wearing warm-ups. The Club only provided jerseys. We wore our own shorts, which were usually the gym shorts that we wore in school for PE. Of course, we were all excited about the idea, but most of us knew that we might not be able to afford a full warm-up, which included the jacket and pants. We then started to discuss what color and what type. The army and navy store called A&N had the warm-ups we liked for about twenty or thirty bucks.

This brought on a lot of anxieties for me. I knew my mother would say no in so many different ways if I was to ask her for the money to buy a warm-up for a basketball game. I started thinking about all the hustling ideas I normally used to get money. One was working over at the coal bin. They paid three cents a bag, but you needed an adult to sign certain papers if you were between thirteen and sixteen. I used to ask my father to sign when Al, Bobby, and I needed money, but my father would ask for half of what we bagged and never lifted a shovel.

Todd and I had several different hustles we would do to make money. One was selling cookies and pastries that his grandfather used to get from a warehouse. They had exceeded the expiration date. His grandfather used to give Todd and his mother boxes of the stuff. His mother gave them away free in the neighborhood while they were still safe to eat. She threatened to kill Todd if she heard that he was selling the cookies and pastries for money.

It was always Todd's idea to sell them, and I would go along, of course. His mother always gave my family a couple of boxes. I never sold the ones given to us. But this time I was really desperate. I tried to get Todd to get some extra boxes to sell, but he said that his mother had found out about us selling some the last time. To this day, I have no idea how Todd's mom would find out about these things. I decided to hold off on this idea and try something else.

I saw Darnell and told him I needed to make some money. He looked at me and asked if I would like to shine some shoes. I said, "Man, you must be crazy, I'm not shining anyone's shoes but mine." I thought it would be very embarrassing standing out in a busy area trying to shine shoes for money. This occupation was always the butt of a lot of jokes. I was already getting teased enough for being poor. But Darnell assured me that we would make a lot of money.

Darnell talked me into shining shoes on Jefferson Avenue between Nineteenth and Twentieth Street. There was a pool hall on this block, and a storefront church and some other businesses. He and I saved our money and purchased a shoe shine kit that was pretty cheap, like a buck or so. We agreed that we would charge twenty-five cents for a shine.

As we were walking to the spot where we were going to shine the shoes, Darnell said that we would have to shout out at those walking by, saying "Shoe shine! Shoe shine for Twenty-five cents!" I said, "There's no way I'm going to do that. What's wrong with just standing here and waiting for customers to come to us? We have signs that say 25 cents a shine." Darnell wasn't the type that argued about anything, so he just agreed. As we were standing there, he started to shout out to those walking by asking if they wanted a shine. The third person walking by decided he would like a shine. After Darnell finished, the gentleman gave him a dollar and told Darnell to keep the change. *Oh, wow!* I thought. He continued with the shouting and got another customer. Once again, the person gave him a dollar and told him to keep the change. By this time I swallowed my pride like a large lump of old chewed-up Bazooka gum and started shouting out like Darnell.

I then got my first customer. As Darnell had found, every customer would leave a tip after they paid the regular cost for the shine. I said to myself, *This is it!* Instead of standing on the corner with my head down hoping that none of my peers would see me, I was standing with my head up high. After about twenty or so customers between us, I started to notice that some guys about three or four years older were peeping around the corner watching us. I turned toward Darnell. Just when I was about to tell him that these guys were checking us out, he said, "I see them," but he just kept asking customers if they wanted a shine. He then said to me just above a whisper, "Sam, when I say let's go, grab your box and run." I just said, "Bet." There were times when the area was not too busy, and I believed these guys were waiting for this break because there would be fewer witnesses. When Darnell bent over as if he was going to get ready for the next shine, he yelled out, "GO!" We took off running. After we were about two blocks away, we looked back and saw the guys walking in the area where we had been standing. Darnell and I decided we would try another day and time. But we never got the nerve to try shining shoes again.

I did at least have enough to buy either the jacket or the top. Now I just needed to find a way to get the rest of the money. Yes, the thought of doing something illegal did cross my mind, but not for long. I just could not see myself surviving in any man's prison; it did not matter if it was only going to be juvenile detention. As our first game approached, Dousey would call or check with everyone to see if they had gotten their warm-up. I would tell him that I was almost there. But about the second week after he mentioned the idea, just about everybody on the team had gotten theirs. The word had gotten out that for the opening game, we were going to be wearing warm-ups.

By this time it was getting close to the first of the month. Although my mother was working at a restaurant, she was making barely a dollar an hour for only maybe twenty-five hours a week. So she was still getting a welfare check. I know they have different names for it today, but this is what we called it back then. Since the first of the month was near; I thought that it might not be a bad idea to ask my mom. I felt that since I had worked for half of the money, maybe she might give me the rest. We knew all our mothers had a secret stash of money just for an emergency. But as far as my mother was concerned, this was not an emergency. It was for me, though. I was starting to imagine me being the only one on the court without a warm-up suit.

I then did something I always hated to do, and that was to ask this gentleman my mom was seeing who was much older than she. She was about thirty-eight, and he was about seventy. I would always ask if she could approach him for me, but she would always tell me to ask for myself. One day I decided to explain my situation to him. Like always, he just smiled and gave me the money.

I immediately got on my bike and rode seventy blocks to the A&N store to purchase my warm-up. I couldn't wait to tell everybody that I finally got my warm-up suit. Of course, when they came around to ask if I had gotten it, I tried to act as if I had the suit for a few days or a week. I then realized just how poor everyone else thought my family and I were compared to everyone else. I always knew that we were financially poorer than everyone else, but as Carolyn always reminded us when I would get teased by everyone else for being poor, "We all live in the projects, and if we were not poor, we would not be living in Dickerson Court." Whenever I told someone on the team that I had gotten my warm-up suit, they would have a look of disbelief on their faces and would always ask me to show them the suit. I was starting to become very annoyed. Some actually thought I had stolen the thing. I decided to not let it bother me too much and just started to look forward to the first game.

The first game of the season was against a team that I mentioned earlier that played us very well. Word had gotten out that both teams would be playing each other on opening night. Everyone knew the Club was going to be packed. We just could not stop talking about the game. On game day, sure enough, it seemed like everybody who lived in East End Newport News was at the Club to see Dousey-n-Em play. Some had already known we were going to be wearing warm-ups—including the other team, who decided to buy their own warm-ups. Their colors were blue with a white stripe down the side of the jacket and pants, while ours were red with a white stripe down the side.

When we came out on the court, you could hear people in the bleachers talking about the warm-ups and how they were impressed with us wearing them. Once again I was reminded how much poorer I was compared to everyone else. As we were warming up when I came close to the bleachers, I heard someone say, "Look, even Sam Reynolds got one on!" They were not saying this to put me down or embarrass me, but they really were surprised that I was able to buy one and were glad to see me in it. I have to admit, annoying as it was, it did keep my head from swelling up.

This game was probably one of the best played at the Club, at least I thought it was. Nard had already said I would start this game. But because of all the anxiety preceding this game, I was starting to get very nervous about playing. Dousey sensed this and told me to relax. By this time there were some who were starting to get tired of us winning every game and really wanted us to lose. Dousey was averaging twenty or more points a game. All the street hustlers were in the middle of the bleachers, with large sums of money folded in their hands placing bets on the game. Of course, they had to be discreet about it because of Pooh Johnson. Right from the start of the game, the crowd was into it. Every single shot from the start, the crowd would cheer very loud, whether either team made the basket or not. Throughout most of the game, both teams traded the lead; there were many times both teams were tied. We did eventually win the game, but with only seconds left on the clock.

We had another undefeated season, drawing what some might call sellout crowds. There was talk about splitting the team up to give another team a chance to win the championship play-offs. But by this time the following year, Dousey had become a basketball star in middle school and went on to become a great ballplayer in high school. Two other players on the team did the same, but they were not as well-known as Dousey. As I mentioned earlier, the area was very competitive, and instead of going through the embarrassment of getting cut from the public school tryouts, the rest of us continued to play for the Club on the senior level (seventeen years old) for different teams. The Club never again drew a sellout crowd like Dousey-n-Em had, but many people after that season looked forward to going to basketball games there. We then played our last softball season together and won the play-off championship again with an undefeated season.

From that point on. the Club really became the place for all young men to go and escape the ills in the inner city. Some of the individuals I grew up with also brought their young children to HRBC and are successful pro athletes to this day. A couple of years later, the Club decided to do something that at that time we thought was a gutsy move. Pooh Johnson and the other directors of the Club decided during the last championship play-off game to let the girls in the neighborhood get two teams together and play one another. This brought the same crowd of spectators as when Dousey-n-Em played. This helped prepare many of us, who had wanted the girls to only come inside the Club to see us play, for what is now the Boys & Girls Clubs of America.

Epilogue

As you can see, my background probably is very similar to most people growing up in the inner city. I decided to share some brief life experiences to help a young reader living in an urban setting see that from trying times, positive lessons can be learned that can help them later in life. It's natural to try to forget about the embarrassing moments. Young men especially only want to remember those experiences they can share later on in life that will demand everyone's respect. But all of us who have grown up in hard times in an urban setting have been in fights, have won some, and have lost some. Most have likely experienced drugs, have gotten in trouble with the law; have experienced sex at an early age, and have seen gang violence that originally started out protecting the neighborhood instead of trying to terrorize it.

It's sad that so many try to instill fear or try to impress people with these experiences, rather than sharing the ones that can be a positive influence in a person's life. What happens is that we end up looking forward to living up to the stereotype that so many people have toward us. Although many of us end up incarcerated from these experiences, there are some who learned valuable lessons from them. I hope that these brief experiences help others going through similar or even harder times to not give up and to take advantage of what's available to you.

We have to remember that today this will impose more of a challenge to those who are raised in low-income housing projects. Most people today feel that all bad habits are ghetto. Or they use ghetto as a byword to represent all badness. When you lie, steal, kill, or use foul language, you're ghetto. Some of the richest people in the world, who never experienced any hard times, have done all these things. I was really ashamed of my background, and most of the time ashamed to discuss it with anyone. But I realized that I was more advanced with life's experiences than some of my peers who were reared in higher-income families.

I knew how to prepare a full-course meal for breakfast, lunch, and dinner before I graduated from high school. I knew how to wash and iron my clothes before I graduated from high school. From watching my mother budget what little money she had to get by, I learned how to be responsible when spending the money I earned. I can go on and on, but when I mention these things to people, they never refer to them as being ghetto. They will tell you that a young person can learn these things growing up in any type of background. And that's exactly my point. As with some of the worst and negative habits a person can learn from a poor background, he can learn some of the best and positive habits as well. The challenge for all is to filter out the worthless ones.

Try to develop a relationship with God early, if there's any organization who truly serves him in truth. Although I never was a member of any church growing up, the basic fundamental Bible truths that I applied in life always benefited me and still do. Every parent I ever knew, even the ones who had serious problems—alcoholics, abusive ones, and drug addicts—always had a positive thought that was in harmony with God. Please listen to this counsel and try your best to apply it during these trying times.

Pay attention to all the good your parents have to offer, even if their education or experience in life may seem to be limited. My mother's math education was about on a fifth-grade level. I learned all she knew about the subject by the time I was in the third grade. So I was two years ahead of a lot of the other students in my class. Math was always easy for me, even algebra, geometry, and calculus—well, the calculus may have caused me some anxieties, but I'm sure you get the point.

The people you choose to closely associate with is important. That includes all associations. For example, take some of the ones I mention throughout this book. I can say in one or two words how each had a positive influence on me. I learned from Carolyn and Sandy how to talk to young ladies; from my sister Pam, how to recognize girls you do not want to give any time of day to. From Todd, I learned ingenuity and why it doesn't pay to lie; from Darnell, how to make honest money; from Possum, how to manage money. I learned from my younger brother Douglas, not to worry about anything; from Dousey, leadership; from Al and Bobby, loyalty. From the Hampton Roads Boys Club (HRBC), I learned unity. From real people in the neighborhood, I learned how to survive, and wisdom. From my mom, I learned patience and how to be a good person to all people. My dad taught me knowledge and the upmost respect I should have for those old enough to be my parents. My relatives taught me why family unity is important. And from God, I learned all of the above and then some.

If there's any recreational facility in the area, really take advantage of what they have to offer to keep you off the streets, and really get to know and help the people in your neighborhood. Never shy away from being creative in a positive way, even if it means losing some friends. If they say you are trying to be white, sometimes it helps to just ignore the comment—or ask why they think only white people can or should be creative. Growing up anywhere can be a challenge for all young people. We all know that there's drugs and violence in all schools and neighborhoods. But we can't ignore the statistical truths about those who grow up in an urban or inner-city setting. Well-paying jobs and families with both parents at home raising children in most cases can protect or allow children to come out victorious over most of the problems facing teens.

Take careful note of these life experiences during your teen years to help you with making important life decisions in the future. Reach out and get to know all the real people in the neighborhood, even the ones you may think are very strange and even if you may have to get teased a little for it. Trust me: I learned a lot from them.

I would like to ask all inner-city youths to look for all the attributes I just listed every time you leave home, when you go to the store, to school, to a sports event whether you are playing or not, the next time you watch a fight whether you are in the fight or not, when looking for a job, when you are pressured to do drugs whether you take the drug or not, every time you spend money, and especially when talking to older people. There will be moments when you may feel like giving up and that you are just not going to make it, but do not give up and try to do your best to change people's expectations and the negative views they have of those who grow up in the inner city in hard times. I assure you that even to this day what I was able to learn from these experiences then is still available today.

Trust me: every neighborhood has its Dousey-n-Em.